I0044769

OPERATION

STRONG SPINE

A BLUE PRINT ON HOW TO SPINE, MONEY & PRODUCTIVITY

PATRICK LEE

Copyright © 2014 by Patrick Lee

Perspectis, Inc.

1 First Canadian Place, Ste. 350

Toronto, ON, Canada M5X 1C1

All rights reserved. No part of this publication may be reproduced, stored in a retrieval system, or transmitted, in any form or by any means, electronic, mechanical, photocopying, recording, or otherwise, without the prior written permission of the author.

ISBN: 978-0-9938841-1-5

Disclaimer: The content of this book is provided for information purposes only, and is not intended to replace the advice and counsel of a professional specialized in the topics covered by this book. The information presented here is not to be considered as complete, nor does it contain all medical, ergonomic, occupational health and safety resource information that may be relevant. All content, including text, graphics, images and information available in this book are for educational purposes only. By reading or using this book, you agree to hold harmless and shall not seek remedy from Patrick Lee or the publisher Perspectis Inc. The author and publisher disclaim all liability to any and all individuals, entities or organizations that use this book for damages, costs, and expenses, including legal fees because of any reliance on anything derived from this book, and furthermore, assume no liability for any and all claims arising out of the said use, regardless of the cause, effect or fault.

DEDICATION

This book is dedicated to my parents, family, colleagues, and back problem sufferers around the world

CONTENTS

PROLOGUE

PART ONE
The Blue Print

PART TWO
Workplace Optimization

ACKNOWLEDGEMENTS

This book didn't come into existence without the generous help and support of many people surrounding me and this book.

My gratitude goes to Dr. Don Fitz-Ritson, Mr. Tony Tocco, and Ms. Janice Yan for their candid reviews, critiques, suggestions, advice and support.

My gratitude also goes to the over 2000 licensed spinal health specialists in United States, Canada, United Kingdom, The Netherlands, Australia, Norway, and another 20 countries, whom I had the honor to serve and work with.

My gratitude also goes to the hundreds of thousands of back and neck pain sufferers around the world, whom I have had the privilege to help with some of my specialized know-how and solutions.

Last but not least, my gratitude goes to the millions of back and neck pain sufferers in the workplaces whom I have yet to have an opportunity to help, but whose suffering and struggle have inspired me to embark on the journey of writing this book in the first place.

PROLOGUE

OPERATION STRONG SPINE

PROLOGUE

1

Why Is The Operation Urgent?

Are you an ergonomist, occupational health and safety specialist, productivity specialist, workplace safety officer, or HR manager? Have your staffs complained to you about their sore backs due to their work, prolonged sitting, or prolonged standing at work? Have they complained to you that the back problems are affecting their productivity at work? Have they asked you to send them to doctors or hospitals for checkups or treatments for their back? Have they missed work days due to their back problems?

If your answer to any of the above questions is yes, you are not alone.

The 2009 National Health Interview Survey (NHIS) indicated that, during a 3-month period alone, 15 percent of the surveyed persons reported having pain in the neck area, and 28 percent reported having pain in the lower back.

According to American Association of Orthopedic Surgeons, 30% or virtually 1 in every 3 American adults are afflicted by back pain each year, which means about 60 – 70 million American adults have had, are experiencing or are going to suffer from back pain within the present calendar year alone.

A study "Lost Productive Time and Cost Due To Common Pain Conditions in the US Workforce" which had a random sample of 28,902 working adults in the United States and was published in JAMA (The Journal of the American Medical Association) in 2003, showed that back pain sufferers lost an average of 5.2 hours of productive time per week.

Back and neck pains are not only pervasive, but also costly to workplace productivity.

According to leading researchers, back pain has literally become a health pandemic in the United States. And the problem is still getting worse.

What's important to realize is that back and neck pains are no longer limited to front line workers. They are increasingly affecting office workers. In fact, sitting has become a leading cause for back pain second only to heavy lifting.

Operation strong spine is urgently needed at workplaces across the country.

2

The Tip of The Iceberg

Back and neck pains are costly. Amongst the 155 million US workforce, an astonishing 1.34 billion productive hours are lost due to back pain in the year of 2010 alone. Furthermore, the lost work hours due to missed workdays counted an additional 101.8 million workdays or 814.4 million hours owing to back pain each year in the US. In total, a whopping 2.154 billions of work hours or 269.3 million workdays are lost to back pain alone in the US each year.

Adding the work hours lost to neck pains, the total work hours lost to back and neck pains quickly approach 2,000 hours or 250 workdays per 100 employees each year, according to World Health Organization Health and Work Performance Questionnaire (HPQ) by R.C. Kessler.

In other words, the grand total of productivity loss to the

problems along the two key areas of the spine, the neck and the back alone, mounts to a mind boggling 3.1 billion work hours or 387.5 million workdays, each year in the US alone.

Assume an average wage of $30/hour, your company would lose close to $60,000 per 100 employees due to back and neck pain each year. Adding an average short-term disability cost of $7,100, an average long-term disability cost of $4,200, and an average workers' compensation cost of $1,900, according to Integrated Benefits Institute, this figure quickly grows to $73,200 per 100 employees per year.

If your company has 1000 employees, your company would have lost 20,000 work hours, 2,500 workdays, and $732,000 a year due to back and neck pains alone.

Yet, the above discussed magnitude productivity losses are only the tip of an iceberg.

3

The Real Pain

Back pain may not be the most frequent pain complaint, but is certainly the most costly pain condition to treat. According to "Relieving Pain in America: A Blueprint for Transforming Prevention, Care, Education, and Research" by Darrell J. Gaskin, Ph.D. and Patrick Richard, Ph.D., M.A, 72.76% of cost for treating all pain conditions in American workplace is attributable to back pain.

OPERATION STRONG SPINE

Conditions	Office Based	Hospital Outpatient	Emergency Services	Hospital Inpatient	Prescription Drugs	Total
Headache	1,350	434	958	147	3,730	6,619
Nonspecific Chest Pain	596	1,040	948	1,930	62	4,576
Abdominal Pain	689	305	438	128	38	1,598
Back Pain	14,400	3,000	607	13,500	2,660	34,167
Total	17,035	4,779	2,951	15,705	6,490	46,960

NOTE: in millions of US$2010, adjusted for inflation as of 2010 using the Medical Care Inflation Index of the Consumer Price Index.
SOURCE: "Relieving Pain in America: A Blueprint for Transforming Prevention, Care, Education, and Research" by Darrell J. Gaskin, Ph.D. and Patrick Richard, Ph.D., M.A,

Yet, most work related back pain and spine problems are preventable. And the prevention of back pain will be the most effective measure in containing the total pain related healthcare costs. One third of reduction in back pain will save companies more money than eliminating most other pain conditions combined.

4

The Real Costs

What is more damaging at workplaces is that the negative effects of absenteeism and presenteeism caused by one individual's back or neck pain doesn't stop with this single person alone. They also affect most others who need to work or collaborate with this person. These people may include the members on the same team, colleagues from other departments, customers, suppliers, investors, even the public in general. As back and neck pains increasingly affect office workers, their negative effects on an organization's productivity has become increasingly far reaching, because the nature of office workers jobs that have higher level of interaction with other parts of the organization.

An important call may be missed, causing decisions or operations in another part of the company to be delayed or

9

carried out incorrectly. A piece of critical data may be entered incorrectly, causing operational mistake at another part of the organization, or a large scale investigation of the whole data system later on. A customer complaint may be left unanswered, leading to a crisis in customer relationship management. Poor mood may affect others in the organization, and may have a longer term consequence on team member relationship which may in turn have a long term repercussion on the team's future productivity.

The absenteeism and presenteeism of one person often spreads their effects throughout the entire organization of your company like the flap of a butterfly's wings, and cause devastating problems or tornado at the other parts of your company, even with your customers, suppliers or investors.

Such impact is difficult to measure, and there is no data available. To access the extent of such damages, one could only use estimation.

Assuming that each minute of absenteeism and presenteeism would cause other employees of your company to lose an average of 0.01 minute, i.e. 0.6 seconds, in their productivity, the overall additional loss of productivity would amount to 2,000 work hours or 250 workdays per 100 employees of your company.

If each minute of absenteeism and presenteeism would cause other employees of your company to lose an average of 0.1 minute, i.e. 6 seconds, in their productivity, the overall additional loss of productivity would amount to 20,000 work hours or 2,500 workdays per 100 employees of your company.

On top of the direct and indirect lost work hours and days, there are the effects of poor quality of work and increased errors by the workers affected by back or neck pains. Such poor quality or work and increased errors may have significant effect of the work hours and days lost.

PROLOGUE

If, for the purpose of simplicity, we ignore the effect of poor quality of work and increased errors, and only focus on the work hours and days lost, a 1% productivity loss due to the direct absenteeism and presenteeism of the worker(s) afflicted by back or neck pains could cause an additional productivity loss of 1% - 10% in your company's overall productivity.

Would it be prudent to estimate that the productivity lost to back and neck pains would be between 2% and 10% in your company's overall productivity?

How important would a recovery of 2-10% of overall productivity be to your company?

How glad would your CEO be when you bring this implication and opportunity to her or him?

How important are you to your company as a workplace safety officer?

Shouldn't you be considered as chief productivity officer of you company?

You are literally the keeper of your company's productivity?

Make no mistake. There is rarely an opportunity that could boost a company's productivity by 2-10%, without investments that are multiple magnitudes higher than the modest investment required for reducing and preventing back and neck pain. Why not jump start your company's Operation Strong Spine today?

OPERATION STRONG SPINE

PART ONE
THE BLUE PRINT

OPERATION STRONG SPINE

1

The Secret to an Effective Blue Print

To develop an effective blue print for Operation Strong Spine, we must first understand what causes back pain and spinal problems. Back pain is one of the most complex health conditions facing humanity, because it can originate from the back, neck, chest, extremities, internal organs, and even the mind. Below is an overview of the various causes.

OPERATION STRONG SPINE

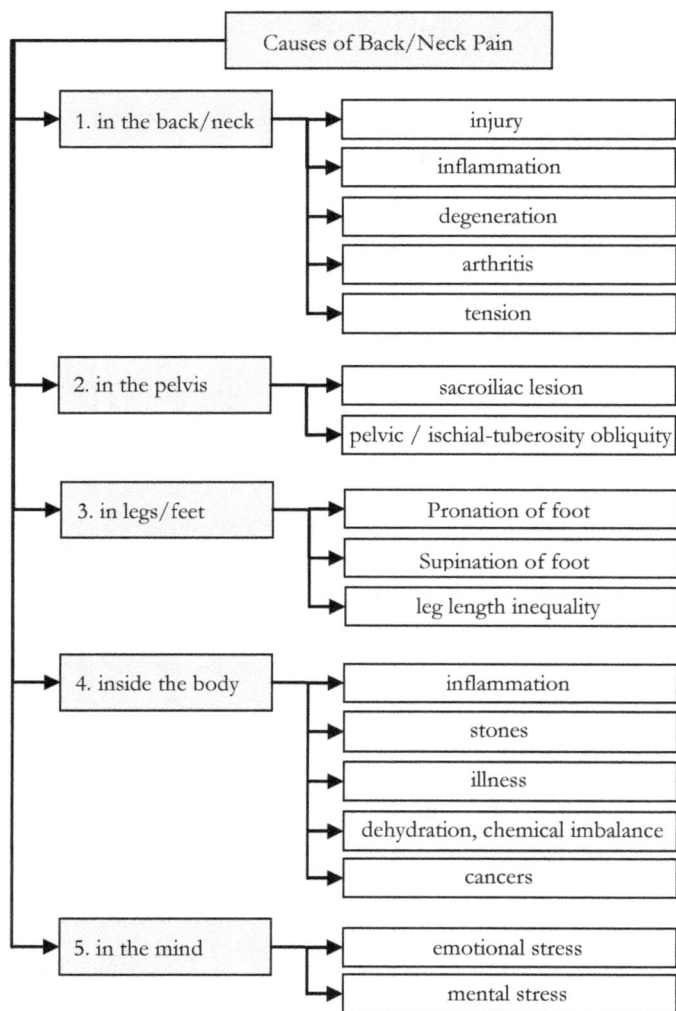

Causes of Back/Neck Pain

1. in the back/neck
- injury
- inflammation
- degeneration
- arthritis
- tension

2. in the pelvis
- sacroiliac lesion
- pelvic / ischial-tuberosity obliquity

3. in legs/feet
- Pronation of foot
- Supination of foot
- leg length inequality

4. inside the body
- inflammation
- stones
- illness
- dehydration, chemical imbalance
- cancers

5. in the mind
- emotional stress
- mental stress

Source: compiled by Patrick Lee

Although there is a wide range of causes for back pain, most back pains at workplaces are not caused by illnesses.

THE BLUE PRINT

Instead, most of them are caused by macro or micro injuries to the musculoskeletal system. And most of them can be prevented.

From above discussion, several important learning become immediately apparent:

1. Multi-disciplinary care and multi-dimensional management are required,
2. Prevention is possible and essential,
3. Ergonomists are the key stakeholders in combating back, neck pain, and other spinal problems at workplaces.

Check #MadBack by Patrick Lee (ISBN: 978-0-9938841-0-8) for further details, if necessary.

2

The Blue Print

Back pain and back injuries are a complex issue. An effective blueprint to combat these problems needs to be multi–dimensional.

All road leads to Rome. However it you don't want to reinvent the wheel, you may consider taking advantage of the following blueprint. It consists of workplace optimization, employee education and training, exercise integration, and operational management.

Naturally, some part of this blueprint may not be entirely suitable to your company's particular situation. Adaptation, modification, or fine tuning will be necessary. This blueprint is provided to help you save some time on your road to develop an effective strategy for combating back and neck

THE BLUE PRINT

pains at your company.

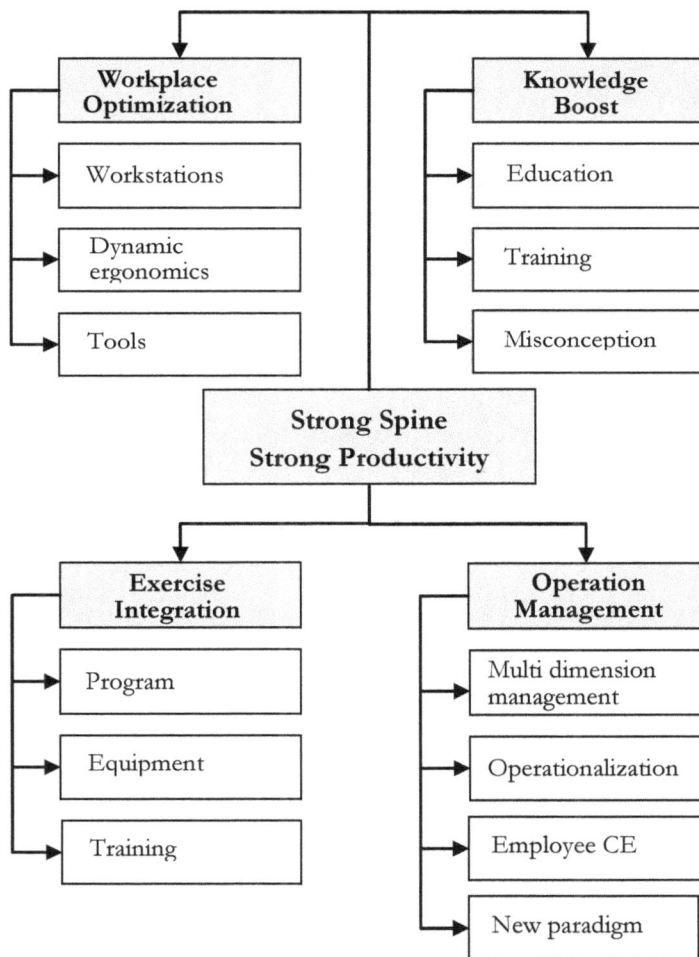

```
┌─────────────────────────────────────┬─────────────────────────────────────┐
│                                                                             │

┌──────────────────────────┐          ┌──────────────────────────┐
│   Workplace              │          │   Knowledge              │
│   Optimization           │          │   Boost                  │
├──────────────────────────┤          ├──────────────────────────┤
│   Workstations           │          │   Education              │
├──────────────────────────┤          ├──────────────────────────┤
│   Dynamic                │          │   Training               │
│   ergonomics             │          │                          │
├──────────────────────────┤          ├──────────────────────────┤
│   Tools                  │          │   Misconception          │
└──────────────────────────┘          └──────────────────────────┘

            ┌──────────────────────────────────┐
            │   Strong Spine                    │
            │   Strong Productivity             │
            └──────────────────────────────────┘

┌──────────────────────────┐          ┌──────────────────────────┐
│   Exercise               │          │   Operation              │
│   Integration            │          │   Management             │
├──────────────────────────┤          ├──────────────────────────┤
│   Program                │          │   Multi dimension        │
│                          │          │   management             │
├──────────────────────────┤          ├──────────────────────────┤
│   Equipment              │          │   Operationalization     │
├──────────────────────────┤          ├──────────────────────────┤
│   Training               │          │   Employee CE            │
└──────────────────────────┘          ├──────────────────────────┤
                                       │   New paradigm           │
                                       └──────────────────────────┘
```

Source: Patrick Lee

OPERATION STRONG SPINE

PART TWO
WORKPLACE
OPTIMIZATION

OPERATION STRONG SPINE

1

Workstations

Workstation review, redesign, or improvement is one of the most important areas of focus in workplace optimization.

Workstations vary from industry to industry, from company to company, and from job to job.

Workstations may include office desks, retail counters, vehicle cockpits, airplane cockpits, assembly lines, material handling spaces, and construction fields.

The workstation is a main factor in determining an employee's posture and behavior, hence, the level of physical stress, at work. Stressors, such as awkward positioning of the body or body part, harmful repetitive motions, vibrations, excessive forces, inadequate lighting, and extreme temperature often leads to unnecessary macro and micro injuries or ergonomic disorders to the back and neck of an employee.

What's important to realize is that the repetitive strains injuries or cumulative trauma disorders caused by repetitive motions are on the rise in the recent decades.

For example, poorly designed workstations often force employees to slouch, such as in the case of sitting in a car seat that provides little or no support to the back, and force the back into a forward facing "C" curve. Or in the case of working in a confined environment, such as underground in a mine, where workers are forced to lay low by bending their back forward. Or in the case of working on something which is positioned relatively low to your head, shoulders, hips or even, knees, such as machining a part, texting on a smart phone, working on a computer, ironing a shirt, cooking a meal, or planting flowers.

While ergonomic design and human factor engineering is a widely applied concept, few workstations are laid out truly ergonomically. This fact becomes immediately apparent if one simply takes a look at the car and airplane seats, or the arrangement of computer keyboards or mice. It is justified to state that the designs of 90% of computer workstations at 90% of North American companies are inadequate in term of their ergonomics.

Workstations are in urgent need of being carefully reviewed and improved.

2

Dynamic Ergonomics

Traditional ergonomics are good, but no longer sufficient.

One of the key purposes of ergonomics is to reduce or prevent repetitive strains on workers. However, more than 90% of ergonomic designs have failed on this objective. Why? Because they have been designed for one static position of the worker or one static relationship between the worker and the system he deals with. However, virtually no worker would remain in the same position during the work, or interact with a working system strictly from one narrow angle or relationship.

Their relationship with the system they deal with is constantly changing. As a result, while ergonomic strains are minimized for one particular position or relationship, they are present even exaggerated in all other positions and relationships which may count up to over 95% of a worker's interactions with the system. In other words, while a system is designed ergonomically for one particular position, it is not ergonomic for most other positions a worker employs during his work.

Examine your own workstation for a moment, in this case it be your desk, chair, computer monitor, key board and mouse. Find and position yourself in the perfection relationship with your system. If your system is ergonomically designed, this would be the most comfortable position and relationship. Now start to perform a variety of normal tasks required by your job, which could be typing a few paragraphs, making a phone call, to looking for a document. And notice how your body's level of comfort changes. Pay attention to all parts of your body, from your hands, arms, legs, buttocks, pelvis, lower back, upper back, to your neck. Did you notice ups and downs of your body's comfort as you perform your tasks? The valley of your comfort curve is where the stress and tensions are. Over time, such stress and tension may lead to repetitive strains injury.

To help resolve this dilemma, modern ergonomics must be dynamic. It must be capable of facilitating, even encouraging, human body's natural need to move, and must adapt and support most, if not each, movement of the body required by work.

Dynamic ergonomics must have the essential abilities to

1. automatically adapt to and support the employee's postures and movements required by their tasks
2. maintain the harmony with the nature of the human body – motion,
3. avoid the static pressure points on the body

WORKPLACE OPTIMIZATION

Why are back problems so pervasive? Reason is rather simple. The artificial world humanity has created for itself is incompatible to the 195,000 years of evolution of our spine and back.

The first line of defense must be the right ergonomics – dynamic ergonomics which is the key to ensure harmony between the human evolution and the industrial revolution.

3

Tools and Equipments

Whether an employee works on a factory floor, at a construction field, or in an office, he or she constantly needs to use a variety of tools, from a hammer, to a shovel, a machine, or a computer mouse.

While some tools and machines have improved a great deal in the recent decades, the ergonomics of many other tools and machines remain primitive. Even worse, the ergonomics of computer systems have virtually remained unchanged since the introduction of personal computers.

This fact will quickly become apparent with a simple 30 second personal experiment:

1. Sit down at your computer desk
2. clear your keyboard and mouse out of your way

WORKPLACE OPTIMIZATION

3. keep your body upright and relaxed
4. drop your hands and arms beside your legs
5. close your eyes and take three deep breaths
6. lift your hands and arms and put them on the desk
7. freeze the positions of your hands and arms
8. open your eyes and look at your hands and arms

Chances are that your arms are pointing to your front with a 45° angle to the center, your thumps are facing upwards also with a 45° angle to the left or right. This is the natural position of your hands and arms. Now compare these positions to the positions of your hands and arms required to work on the computer keyboards or operate a mouse. You will notice a significant difference.

You will notice that computer keyboards and the process will force your arms to be stretched out in parallel and your hands will be forced to rotate inward, and upwards creating a misalignment between your hand and arm.

Same as workstations, tools and equipments used by employee everyday also need an urgent review and upgrade.

OPERATION STRONG SPINE

PART THREE
KNOWLEDGE BOOST

OPERATION STRONG SPINE

1

Education

No matter how well your workstations, tools and equipments are ergonomically designed, the postural stresses and biomechanical damages will continue to negatively affect your employee's body, if they don't use these equipments correctly or if they don't know how to use his own body correctly.

One of the key causes for biomechanical tension, stress and damages is the lack of knowledge or poor habit.

For example, many people slouch when working in front of a computer, walk or stand with their heads leaned forward, or some people walk or stand, with their chest closed and their shoulders rolled forward. Or they lift heavy objects without keeping the object close to their body or without holding a deep breath.

Most employees don't have a clear understanding about the causes of most common back and neck pains. Most of them lack adequate level of sensitivity or awareness for their poor body mechanics.

Most of them have critical misunderstanding about back and neck pains that often leads to unnecessary injury or exaggeration of the pain.

Employees urgently need to be educated on:

1. What causes back and neck pain
2. Key natures of the back, neck and spine
3. Right lifestyles
4. Right work styles

Workers need to become their own first line of defense. After all, initial warning signals could only be sensed by the affected individual themselves. Workers must be educated and trained to be able to identify early warning signals and take proactive measures and appropriate first response to protect themselves and to improve their work practices, conditions, or places.

2

Training

Understanding the "what" and the "why" is important. However, workers also need to understand and experience the "how".

Workshops can be organized. Experts can be brought in. Employee experience sharing can be extremely beneficial.

Proper training shall help workers to realize:

1. How to use their workstations
2. How to work in their environment
3. How to better use their tools and equipment

And in general...
1. How to sit healthily

OPERATION STRONG SPINE

2. How to lift safely
3. How to properly look at the computer screens
4. How to effectively detect early warning signals

3

Misconceptions

A large number of misconceptions exist about back pain that are detrimental to workers in the prevention and recovery of their back and neck problems.

Go through the following list, to see whether your employees have any of them. If they do, help them clarify why the misunderstandings are faulty. Help them put these misconceptions behind.

The top misconceptions that employees have about back and neck pain include:

1.   Look, my back pain is gone. I am all cured now!

OPERATION STRONG SPINE

2. Bed rest is good for recovery from back pain.

3. Sitting in a chair helps recovery from back pain.

4. Movement could worsen your back pain.

5. Severe back pain can paralyze my spine.

6. I have back pain, it must mean that there is something seriously wrong with me.

7. Taking pain killers is the way to solve the problem.

8. Visiting my family doctor should be the first thing to do when hit by back pain.

9. Conventional medicine is more effective than non-conventional medicine.

10. Cold/heat pack, massage, and topical creams relieve back pain, they must help cure the problem.

11. If I don't lift heavy objects, back pain won't afflict me.

12. I have an expensive chair at work; so I won't be hit by back pain.

13. I know how to walk in high heels, so I won't have back pain.

14. I am muscular and strong; back pain won't hit me.

KNOWLEDGE BOOST

15. I exercise regularly; back pain won't hit me.

16. I am a tough guy. Back pain is nothing to be worried about. I will be able to take it.

17. Back pain is a thing for older people. I am young and don't need to worry about it.

18. Back pain is inherited, no one in my family has it, therefore I won't have it.

19. I am young, spinal degeneration won't happen to me.

20. Intensity of back pain correlates with the level of damage to my back.

21. X-ray, MRI, or CT scans can tell what causes my back pain.

22. I am hit by back pain, I'd better change or stay away from work.

23. Chronic back pain is caused by stress or depression. The pain will stop once stress or depression is resolved.

24. Back pain often leads to disability.

25. If no physical or pathological cause is found, I must have a psychological issue that causes back pain.

26. I have to live with my back pain for the rest of my life.

27. Surgery is the ultimate cure for back pain.

28. Severe back pain indicates that I need surgery.

29. Prolonged, chronic back pain indicates that I need surgery.

30. If nothing else works, I need surgery.

31. Poor posture, body mechanics and spinal alignment do not always cause back pain, therefore I don't need to pay attention to my posture, body mechanics and spinal alignment.

32. Big and cushy executive chairs are good for your back.

33. Chiropractic is dangerous.

34. Fluffy sleeping pillows are good.

35. Soft mattresses are good for your back.

PART FOUR
EXERCISE INTEGRATION

OPERATION STRONG SPINE

1

Programs

Warm up and distress exercises are amongst the most important measures in preventing unnecessary back and neck pain.

The body of a professional athlete is like a piece of superb equipment. Yet, they still need adequate warm up exercises before each training or competition. Professional marshal artists and acrobat performers train their bodies like well oiled machines. Yet, they still need ample warm up exercises before each performance. Professional speakers have tongue as flexible as snakes. Yet, they still need to do tongue, mouth and vocal warm ups before each speech. Employees are the performers at their own workstations, and should be no exception.

OPERATION STRONG SPINE

There is a great number of exercises available. For your convenience, some of the simple and effective warm up exercises for neck and back are listed in the appendix at the end of this book.

These exercises are not only beneficial at the beginning of the work day, but also during and at the end of the work day.

Regular exercises also help restore the strength of the back and neck.

A 3 minute warm up or distress routine before, during and after the work will make a world of the difference.

It is important not to overdo yourself. You must progress gradually. Take on one exercise at a time. Starting from the most gentle ones.

If any exercise gives you any sharp pain in the back or legs, stop it immediately, and switch to another one. Sharp pains are often related to exaggeration of a fresh wound or pinched nerve. Little or no benefit could be gained by exaggerating a wound or pinching a nerve unnecessarily.

If any exercise gives you any deeper pain (instead of the muscle sore that one often get after a good session of exercises) that remains severe after a night of sleep, you also need to stop doing it immediately.

If you don't have any back pain and simply want to do something to prevent it, you are most likely not to experience any sharp or deep pain in the back or legs. However, you still need to begin with the most gentle ones first and take on no more than one new exercise each day. And always practice the general exercise precautions.

Exercises are to be adjusted by the nature of the work and the condition of the workers.

Consult a qualified advisor in case of any questions.

2

Equipment

Equipment that a workplace needs are mainly those designed to help employees do warm up and distress exercises.

Stretching, balancing, and reaction exercise equipments are highly beneficial.

Also highly beneficial are equipment to help employees do counter-routine motions or posture. Counter-routine motions refer to those motions and posture that are in reversal to the common movements and posture required by an employee's work. Counter-routine exercises are amongst the most effective measures an employee can take to distress the body.

For example, counter-routine motion for an employee who is always on her feet may be backward walking or sitting, while a counter-routine posture for the same person may be head-down hand stand or feet hanging. The counter-routine motion for an employee who spends hours working at a computer, a counter-routine motion may be standing, walking, or jumping, while a counter-routine posture for the same person may be torso extension.

Strength equipment and cardio equipment would be secondary at work places.

3

Training

Help employees exercise the right way is the key. To this end, it is also critical to help employees understand the specific purpose of a particular exercise that they are recommended to do. They also need to understand why these exercises can help them. Such understanding will help them do the exercises the right way long after their initial trainging periods have past. Such understanding will also motivate them to continue the exercise routines long after initial curiosity and enthusiasm have past.

Trainers can be involved. Training manuals can be provided. And exercise apps can be implemented.

OPERATION STRONG SPINE

PART FIVE
OPERATIONAL
MANAGEMENT

OPERATION STRONG SPINE

1

Operationalization

The factors that stress and damage the back and neck are constantly at work for your employees. Your company's fight against these factors must also be constantly at work.

The only way to assure continuity and consistency of your fight is to operationalize your effort, to have it integrated in the daily operational procedure of your employees, to have specific time allocated to it, and to have its performance monitored and measured. Such measures can be integrated with your other workplace safety programs.

For example, warm up time could be planned in work time, warm up exercises could be made mandatory before beginning formal work, besides each signage for wearing eye protection, a sign on lifting safety could be placed.

2

Multidimensional Management

From the above discussion, it is apparent that combating back and neck pain is far more than organizing a few lunch and learn sessions for the employees.

A multidimensional management approach and system are required. The multidimensional approach must include such essential elements as workplace optimization, employees education, exercise integration, and operationalization of the management system.

Centrally coordinated efforts in these areas are critical. Proper planning, coordination, and operationalization are the keys in the fight against back and neck pain, and the related productivity losses.

3

Employee CE

What not reminded will be forgot
What not refurbished will be confused
What not measured will be ignored

Professionals from doctors to accountants are required to enroll in continuing educational programs and obtain credits. Why not employees of a company? After all, employees are the most critical assets of a company. Wouldn't it make sense to establish routine maintenance for your employees as you do for your machineries?

Such EC can be integrated with the CE programs of your company's other continuing education programs.

4

New Paradigm

We know that old status quo is not working. However, above discussed measure will not be effective unless a new paradigm is established amongst the workers in your company. A new paradigm is urgently needed.

But what should this new paradigm be, to be able to meet the challenges of the new age? No one has the silver-bullet. However, based on our discussion in the previous chapters, the following essential elements are required for this new paradigm.

1. Realize the Vulnerability of the Spine

Many people have been told that the spine is one of the strongest parts of our body. However, the staggering statistics that 30% of adult Americans are afflicted by back pain each year indicates the contrary. The fact that the spine doesn't easily fall apart doesn't mean that it is not vulnerable. Without realizing its vulnerability, appropriate care and maintenance that it deserves become illusions, and unnecessary injury and pain become logical outcomes.

Stop thinking the spine is one of the strongest parts of the body will help employees stop taking their back and neck for granted, and prevent back and neck problems.

2. Realize the Importance of the Spine

A healthy spine doesn't just mean that an employee will be pain free. In fact, everything is on top of it, from the employee's wellbeing, productivity and satisfaction, to your company's overall moral, effectiveness and profitability. Everything is at stake.

Give the spine the credit that is long overdue. Appreciate the spine more. Learn more about it. Do more for it. Be more careful when using it.

3. Take Care of the Spine as You Do with Your Teeth

What is in your spine is far more important than what in your teeth.

Unfortunately, despite such critical importance, most people take far less care of their neck and back, than of their teeth.

Take more care of the spine. Give at least the same, if not doubled, amount of attention, effort, and resources for your spine as for your teeth.

4. Demand Cross Discipline Collaboration

In the past century, not only conventional medical sciences

have made great progresses in spinal health. The medical sciences and arts of many other disciplines of healthcare have also made great progresses. There is a new balance of competence amongst the various healthcare disciplines for spine health.

Specialists must realize the limitation of their own discipline of care, and appreciate the strength of other disciplines of care for spinal health diagnosis and treatment. Corporations must demand that they actively seek opinions of their colleagues from other disciplines of care in helping their employees with back or neck issues.

5. Adopt New Healthy Lifestyles and Habits

We all know that right habits and lifestyle are critical. What most people may not appreciate enough is the fact that sitting is the new smoking. Sitting is a leading cause for occurrence, exaggeration and repetition of back injuries and pain.

The culprit of sitting for back problems is physical inactivity in the back, along with slouching. Help your sedentary employees breakdown the physical inactivity while sitting. Static ergonomics can't meet this demand. However, Dynamic Ergonomics can offer solutions. Find ways to keep the motion in your employees' backs while sitting.

6. Integrate prevention at workplaces

Prevention must be given higher priority in spinal health management.

One ounce of prevention is worth a pound of cure for patients. At workplace, one ounce of prevention would be worth a pound of productivity, healthcare expenditure, and profitability.

PART SIX
JOIN THE MOVEMENT

OPERATION STRONG SPINE

1

Join the Movement

The new dawn is up us now. Be a leader of the new dawn.

The artificial environment is increasingly in conflict with human body's natural needs and wellbeing.

Back and neck pains are increasing, and is increasingly affecting productivities and workplaces.

Employees are increasingly demanding for protection of their wellbeing at workplaces.

Actively paying attention to and taking care of your employees' back and neck health is a matter of "when" instead of "if".

The earlier you begin Operation Strong Spine, the more you will reap its benefits.

2

Key Success Factors

Back and neck pain are complex issues. Your approach must be comprehensive too.

Key success factors for your Operation Strong Spine include:

1. Dynamic ergonomics
2. Multi dimensional management approach and system
3. Prevention is the savior
4. Operationalization
5. New paradigm

3

Need Help?

Call us! We are only one call away. It will be our privilege to assist you.

Email us at advice@OperationStrongSpine.com

Call us at 416-595-1575

Check out #MadBack (ISBN: 978-0-9938841-0-8) if you would need to learn more about the secrets of the spine and its health.

OPERATION STRONG SPINE

APPENDIX I
EXERCISES FOR THE NECK

OPERATION STRONG SPINE

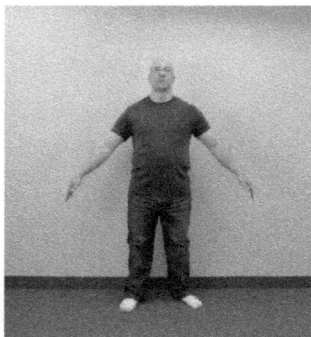

Exercise 1 (Open Chest with Arms to the Side)

- Stand upright with two hands naturally dropped at both sides of the body, and two feet separated in shoulder distance.
- Gently lift your arms and hands to a 45 degree angle with hands aligned with the arms, and the palms facing down.
- Rotate your palm forward.
- Move your hands and arms backward, and roll your shoulders backward to open your chest at the same time.
- Rotate your head to the left as much as you can, when your hands and shoulders can't move further backward. Hold at this position and count 1 to 10.
- Gently return to your neutral standing position.
- Repeat the same motion with your head rotate to the right.
- 6 repetitions at a time.

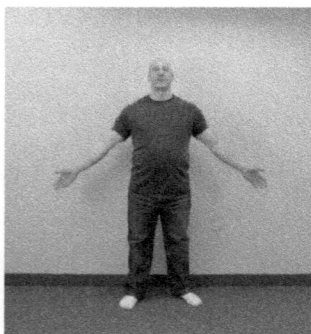

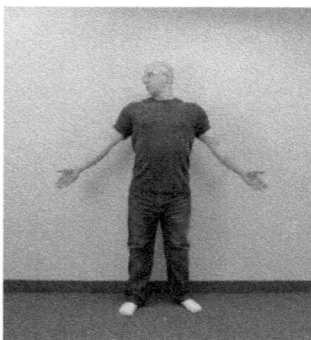

EXERCISES FOR THE NECK

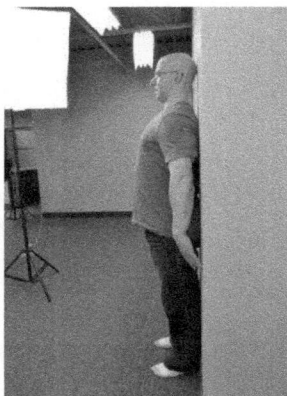

Exercise 2 (Standing Back Wall Press)
- Stand against a straight wall, while making sure that your buttocks are in touch with the wall.
- Gently move your feet backward to touch the wall.
- Gently extend your shoulder to touch the wall.
- Gently move your head backward to touch the wall, while keeping your chin back as much as you can.
- Hold for 8 seconds by counting the numbers 2001 and 2002, 2003, 2004, 2005 and 2006.
- Relax.
- 20 repetitions each day.

Exercise 3 (Standing Wall Push Up)
- Stand facing a wall at arm's length.
- Gently raise your arm to touch the wall, with your hands and rest your body against the wall.
- Gently bend your arms and push your chest closer to the wall.
- Hold for 8 seconds by counting the numbers 2001 and 2002, 2003, 2004, 2005 and 2006.
- Gently straighten your arms and return to neutral position.
- 20 repetitions each day.

Exercise 4 (Standing Head Side to Side Tilt)

- Stand upright.
- Gently bend your head to your left, while facing forward as much as you can.
- Hold for 5 seconds by counting the numbers 2001 and 2002, 2003 and 2004.
- Gently and slowly return to neutral position.
- Repeat the same motion to your right.
- 20 repetitions a day.

Exercise 5 (Standing Head Front to Back Tilt)

- Stand upright.
- Gently bend your head forward as much as you can..
- Hold for 5 seconds by counting the numbers 2001 and 2002, 2003 and 2004.
- Gently and slowly return to a neutral position.
- Repeat the same motion by bending your head backward.
- 20 repetitions a day.

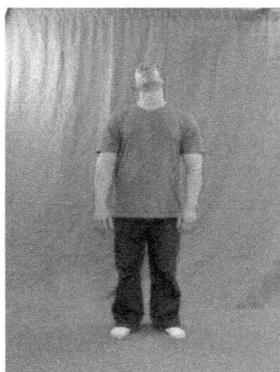

Exercise 6 (Standing Head Rotations)

- Stand upright.
- Gently rotate your head clockwise first toward your right, then your front, then your left, then your back or rear, then …
- Gently return to your neutral position of standing upright.
- Gently rotate your head counter-clockwise first toward your left, then your front, then your right, then your rear, then …
- Gently return to your neutral position of standing upright.
- 20 repetitions a day.

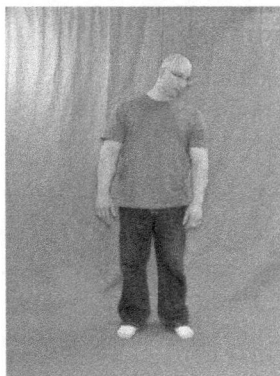

OPERATION STRONG SPINE

Exercise 7 (Standing Side to Side Head Rotation)
- Stand upright.
- Gently rotate your head to your left.
- Gently return to your neutral position of standing upright.
- Gently rotate your head to your right.
- Gently return to your neutral position of standing upright.
- 20 repetitions a day.

Exercise 8 (Standing Side to Side Head Resistance Press)
- Stand or sit upright.
- Gently press your left hand on the left head.
- Gently bend your head to your left, while applying resistance with your left hand.
- Gently return to your neutral position of standing upright.
- Gently repeat the same motion to your right with your right hand as resistance.
- 20 repetitions a day.

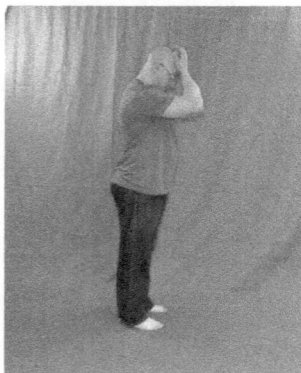

Exercise 9 (Standing Front Resistance Head Press)
- Stand or sit upright.
- Gently press you hands on your forehead.
- Gently push your head forward, while applying resistance with your hands.
- Gently return to your neutral position of standing or sitting upright.
- 20 repetitions a day.

EXERCISES FOR THE NECK

Exercise 10 (Standing Backward Resistance Head Press)

- Stand or sit upright.
- Gently press your hands on the back of your head.
- Gently push your head backward, while applying resistance with your hands.
- Gently return to your neutral position of standing or sitting upright.
- 20 repetitions a day.

Exercise 11 (Standing Resistance Head Rotation)

- Stand or sit upright.
- Gently press your hands on your left face and jaw.
- Gently rotate your head toward your left, while applying resistance with your left hand.
- Gently return to your neutral position of standing or sitting upright.
- Gently repeat the same motion to your right with your right hand.
- 20 repetitions a day.

Exercise 12 (Standing Reverse Arm Stretch)

- Stand or sit upright.
- Gently raise your arms, with your upper arms being horizontal.
- Gently stretch your upper arms horizontally backward.
- Hold for 8 seconds by counting the numbers 2001 and 2002, 2003, 2004, 2005 and 2006.
- Gently return to your neutral position of standing or sitting upright, but with your arms raised.
- 20 repetitions a day.

OPERATION STRONG SPINE

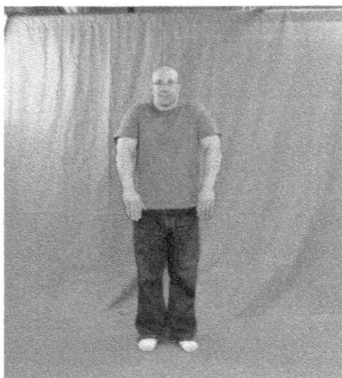

Exercise 13 (Standing Shrugs)
- Stand upright.
- Gently raise your shoulders and rotate them forward, then downward, then backward, then upward.
- Gently reverse the motion by rotating your shoulders backward, then downward, then forward, then upward.
- 20 repetitions a day.

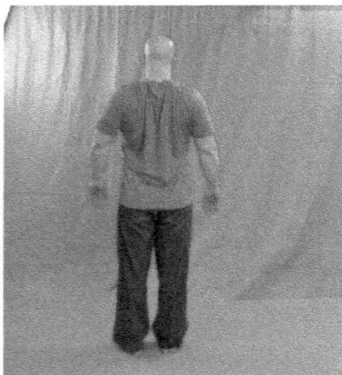

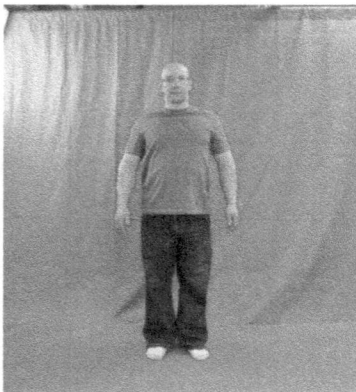

EXERCISES FOR THE NECK

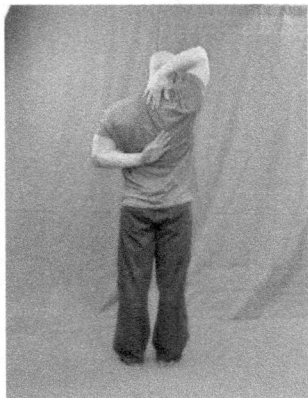

Exercise 14 (Behind the Back Arm Reach)
- Stand upright.
- Gently raise your right arm and bend it to your back over your right shoulder, while bending your left arm to your back from the left side of your lumbar area.
- Gently move your hands towards each other as much as you can.
- Hold for 8 seconds by counting the numbers 2001 and 2002, 2003, 2004, 2005 and 2006.
- Gently straighten your arms and return to a neutral position.
- Repeat the some motion with reversed arms.
- 20 repetitions each day.

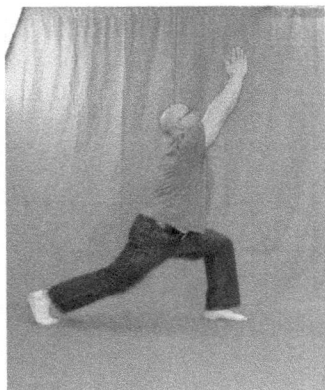

Exercise 15 (Candle Pose)
- Stand upright.
- Gently take a large step forward, with your left foot and lower your body.
- Gently extend your arms forward and upward with your hands touching each other and pointing the mid day sun, as if there is an invisible string between your fingers and the sun pulling your body upward.
- Hold for 8 seconds by counting the numbers 2001 and 2002, 2003, 2004, 2005 and 2006.
- Gently return to a neutral position.
- 20 repetitions each day.

OPERATION STRONG SPINE

APPENDIX II
EXERCISES FOR THE BACK

OPERATION STRONG SPINE

Exercise 1 (Upward Fingers-Jointed Lift with Overhead Stretch)

- Stand upright with two hands naturally dropped at both sides of the body, and two feet separated in shoulder distance.

- Gently lift and joint your hands and fingers in front of your body, with your palms facing up.

- Lift your hand up with fingers jointed.

- Rotate your palms outward to the front when your hands reached your chest level.

- Push your hands upward with your fingers jointed. Your eye should follow your hands from your eye level upwards.

- When your hands push to the highest point, hold at that position and count 1 to 10.

- Gently return to your neutral standing position.

- 6 repetitions at a time.

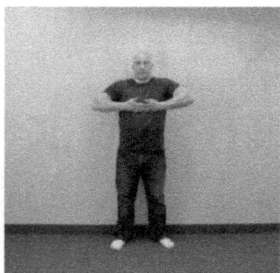

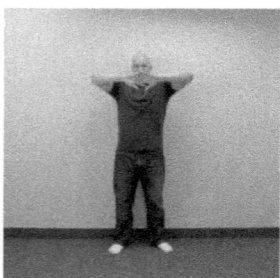

EXERCISES FOR THE BACK

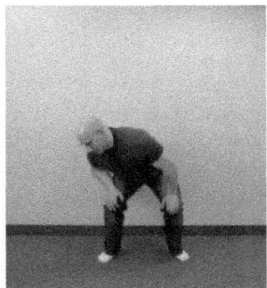

Exercise 2 (Squat with Circular Torso Motion)

- Stand upright with two hands naturally dropped at both sides of the body, and two feet separated in one and a half shoulder width.

- Gently bend your knees and place your hands on your corresponding knees.

- Gently shift your back and head forward to the lift, while holding your knees, hands and buttocks still.

- Continue to shift your head and back towards the middle with your head pointing the front, while holding your knees, hands and buttocks still.

- Continue shift your head and back towards the right, while holding your knees, hands and buttocks still.

- Continue to shift your head and back backwards with your head pointing up and slightly to the back, while holding your knees, hands and buttocks still.

- Repeat this motion in the reversed direction.

- 6 repetitions at a time.

- Return to neutral position when desired repetitions are completed.

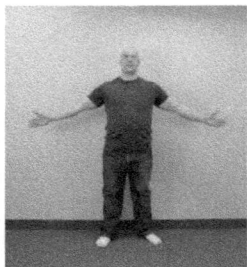

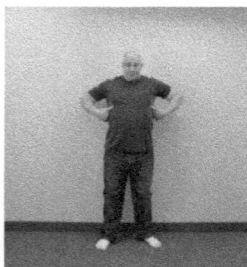

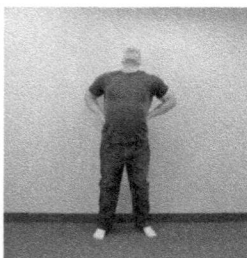

Exercise 3 (Hands behind back with "C" Curve Stretch)

- Stand upright with two hands naturally dropped at both sides of the body, and two feet separated in one and a half shoulder width.
- Gently lift your arms up from the sides of your body till they both pointing upward in parallel.
- Bend your arms and lower your hands, with your elbows pointing to the sides of your body.
- Your upper arm stop moving once your upper arms and forearms come into one line in parallel to your shoulder line.
- Continue to move your hands down and backwards to grab and wrap your upper body.
- Push your hands downwards along your body till they reach the pelvis bones at the back of your waist.
- Push on your pelvis bone from behind with your hands as hard as you can, and stretch your head and upper body upwards as much as you possibly can.
- Hold and count from 1 to 10 once your body is stretched to the maximum.
- Gently return to neutral position.
- 6 repetitions at a time.

EXERCISES FOR THE BACK

Exercise 4 (Standing Side to Side Shifts)
- Bend your arms behind your head.
- Gently bend your body toward the left.
- Gently return to a neutral position.
- Gently continue to bend toward the right.
- Gently return to a neutral position.
- Meanwhile face forward and keep your pelvis horizontal.
- 20 repetitions a day.

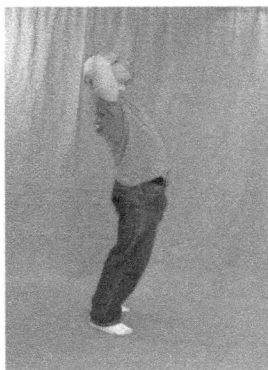

Exercise 5 (Standing Front to Back Tilts)
- Bend your arms behind your head.
- Gently bend your body backwards.
- Gently return to a neutral position.
- Gently continue to bend forward.
- Gently return to a neutral position.
- Meanwhile keep your legs and pelvis stable.
- 20 repetitions a day.

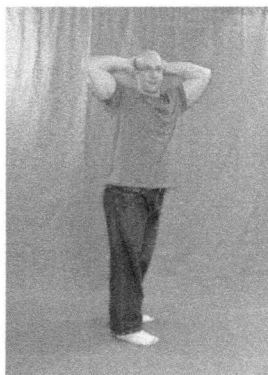

Exercise 6 (Standing Side to Side Rotations)
- Bend your arms behind your head.
- Gently rotate your body towards the right.
- Gently return to a neutral position.
- Gently continue to rotate your body toward left.
- Gently return to a neutral position.
- Meanwhile keep your legs and pelvis stable.
- 20 repetitions a day.

OPERATION STRONG SPINE

Exercise 7 (Walking Side to Side Rotations)

- Walk in large steps straight forward.
- Gently swing arms and upper body in opposite directions of the forward foot.
- Gently swing upper body and arms to right when left foot moves forward.
- Gently return to a neutral position.
- Gently continue to swing upper body and arms to the left when right foot moves forward.
- Gently return to a neutral position.
- Walk 100 steps this way each day.

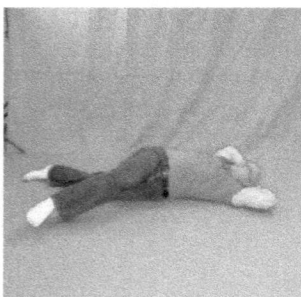

Exercise 8 (Lying Side to Side Rotations)

- Gently lie down on your back on the floor.
- Bend your arms behind your head.
- Gently raise your right foot and leg straight up.
- Gently turn your raised right foot and leg to the left.
- Gently continue to reach out to the left with the tip of your right foot, as much as you can.
- Gently return to a neutral position while keeping your right leg raised.
- Gently lower your right leg and foot to the floor.
- Repeat same motion with left leg and foot.
- 20 repetitions a day.

EXERCISES FOR THE BACK

Exercise 9 (Lying Cat Stretch)

- Kneel on all fours while keeping your torso straight and your head aligned with your spine.
- Lift your lower and mid back as high as you can, like a cat, to make your back to form an arc.
- Gently shift your torso backward while keeping your lower and mid back lifted up as much as you can.
- Gently lower your shoulders while still keeping your lower and mid back lifted up as much as you can, like a cat stretches herself. Don't lift your head, continue to keep your head aligned with your spine.
- Gently move your torso forward while keeping your shoulders and body as low as you can without touching the floor, as if you were creeping forward and don't want to be detected, again like a cat.
- When your shoulders reach the position directly above your hands, you start to slowly push up your body with your arm. However, your torso may continue to move forward to its maximum. In this process, your head moves as if continuously pulled by the mid day sun and along a "c" curve that opens upward.
- When your arms stretch to their fullest, you begin to lift your waist and slowly move your torso backward. Try to lift your lower and mid back as high as possible, to make your back form an arc.
- 20 repetitions each day.

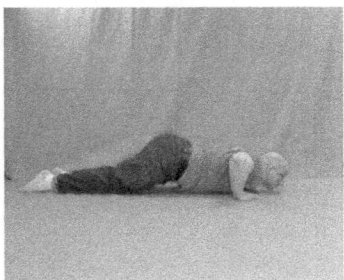

Exercise 10 (Seated Cross Body Reach)

- Sit on the floor with legs crossed.
- Gently raise your right knee and point your right foot forward.
- Gently pull your left leg to the right while keeping it close to you.
- Gently extend your left arm toward your right and pass your right knee.
- Continue gently rotating your torso toward the right to the maximum you can. (well practiced individuals are able to rotate the torso until the left shoulder passes your raised right knee.)
- Hold for 5 seconds by counting the numbers 2001 and 2002, 2003 and 2004.
- Very gently and slowly return to neutral position with legs crossed.
- Continue in the reversed direction...
- Gently raise your left knee and point your left foot forward.
- Gently pull your right leg to the left while keeping it close to you.
- Gently extend your right arm toward your left and pass your left knee.
- Continue gently rotating your torso toward the left to the maximum you can. (well practiced individuals are able to rotate the torso until the right shoulder passes your raised left knee.)
- Hold for 5 seconds by counting the numbers 2001 and 2002, 2003, and 2004.
- Very gently and slowly return to neutral position with legs crossed.
- 10 repetitions each day.

EXERCISES FOR THE BACK

Exercise 11 (Kneeling Arm Reach)

- Kneel on all fours, while keeping your torso straight and your head aligned with your spine.
- Gently extend your left arm forward and extend your right leg backward, while maintaining your body balance with your right hand and left knee on the floor.
- Gently return to the neutral position of being on all fours.
- Repeat same motion with extending right arm and left leg.
- 20 repetitions a day.

Exercise 12 (Knelling Leg Lift)

- Kneel on all fours, while keeping your torso straight and your head aligned with your spine.
- Gently extend your right leg backward while maintaining your body balance with your two hands and left knee on the floor.
- Gently return to the neutral position of being on all fours.
- Repeat same motion with extending left leg.
- 20 repetitions a day.

Exercise 13 (Standing Backward Leg Lift)

- Stand up straight.
- Gently extend both of your hands and arms forward.
- Gently lift your right leg backward, while maintaining your body balance on your left foot on the floor.
- Gently return to the neutral position of standing up straight.
- Repeat same motion with lifting your left leg backward, while maintaining your body balance on your right foot on the floor.
- 20 repetitions a day.

81

OPERATION STRONG SPINE

Exercise 14 (Standing Torso Rotations)
- Stand upright.
- Bend your arm behind your head.
- Gently rotate your torso clockwise first toward your right, then your front, then your left, then your rare, then ...
- Gently return to your neutral position of standing upright.
- Gently rotate your torso counter-clockwise first toward your left, then your front, then your right, then your rear, then ...
- Gently return to your neutral position of standing upright.
- 20 repetitions a day.

82

EXERCISES FOR THE BACK

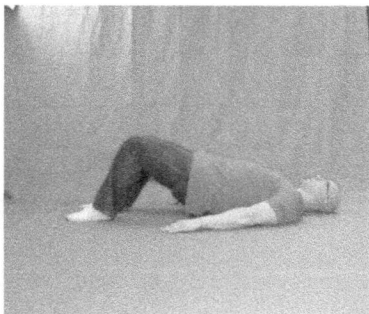

Exercise 15 (Lying Butt Lift)
- Lie down on your back.
- Gently raise your knees and pull your feet close your buttocks.
- Gently raise your pelvis as much as you can by pushing on the floor with your feet.
- Hold for 5 seconds by counting the numbers 2001 and 2002, 2003 and 2004.
- Gently lower your buttocks on the floor.
- 20 repetitions a day.

Exercise 16 (Lying Pelvis and Leg Lifts)
- Lie down on your back.
- Gently raise your right knee and pull your right foot close your buttocks.
- Gently raise your pelvis as much as you can by pushing into the floor with your right foot, while keeping your left leg in line with your torso.
- Hold for 5 seconds by counting the numbers 2001 and 2002, 2003 and 2004.
- Gently lower your buttocks and your left leg and foot back on the floor.
- Gently raise your left knee and pull your left foot close your buttocks.
- Gently raise your pelvis as much as you can by pushing on the floor with your left foot, while keeping your right leg in line with your torso.
- Hold for 5 seconds by counting the numbers 2001 and 2002, 2003 and 2004.
- Gently lower your buttocks and your right leg and foot back on the floor.
- 20 repetitions a day.

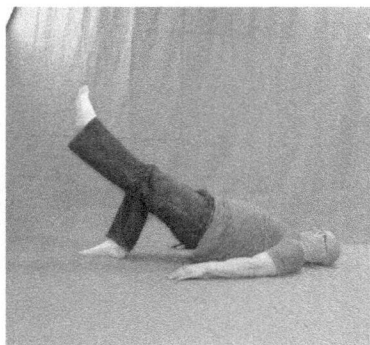

OPERATION STRONG SPINE

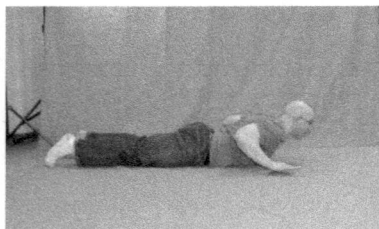

Exercise 17 (Lying Breaststrokes)

- Lie down on your stomach.
- Gently raise your head to face forward, while lifting your shoulders up and extending your arms and hands forward.
- Gently and slowly pull back your arms and hands in circular motion as if you are swimming breaststroke.
- Extend your arms and hands forward once they are back to your shoulder level.
- Repeat the circular breaststroke motions while keeping your shoulders and head up.
- 20 repetitions a day.

EXERCISES FOR THE BACK

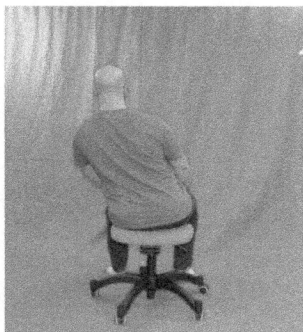

Exercise 18 (Seated Body Shifts)
- Sit upright.
- Gently shift your shoulders toward your left, while keeping your buttocks stable and your pelvis as horizontal as possible.
- Hold for 5 seconds by counting the numbers 2001 and 2002, 2003 and 2004.
- Gently and slowly return to your upright neutral position.
- Gently reverse the motion by shifting your shoulders toward your right, while keeping your buttocks stable and your pelvis as horizontal as possible.
- Hold for 5 seconds by counting the numbers 2001 and 2002, 2003 and 2004.
- Gently and slowly return to your upright neutral position.
- 20 repetitions a day.

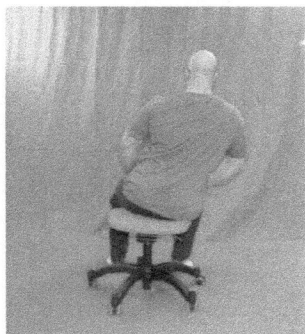

Exercise 19 (Seated Side to Side Bending)
- Sit upright.
- Bend your arms behind your head.
- Gently bend your back toward your right, while keeping your buttocks stable and your pelvis horizontal.
- Hold for 5 seconds by counting the numbers 2001 and 2002, 2003 and 2004
- Gently and slowly return to your upright neutral position.
- Gently repeat same motion by bending your back toward your left.
- 20 repetitions a day.

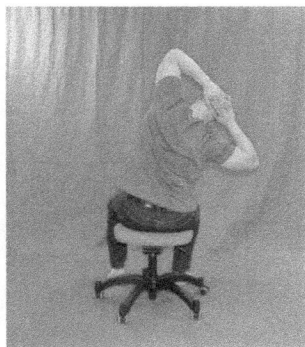

Exercise 20 (Seated Forward Hip Bending)
- Sit upright.
- Gently bend your torso forward and reach the floor with your hands, if possible.
- Hold for 5 seconds by counting the numbers 2001 and 2002, 2003 and 2004.
- Gently and slowly raise your head and let your head pull up your spine vertebra by vertebra, as if pulling up a string of beats by one of its ends.
- Hold for 5 seconds by counting the numbers 2001 and 2002, 2003 and 2004.
- 20 repetitions a day.

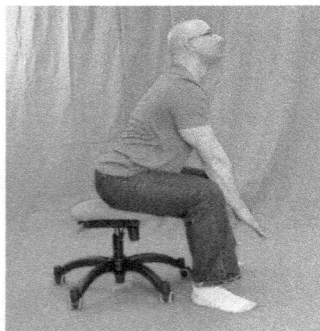

Exercise 21 (Seated Torso Twists)
- Sit upright.
- Gently twist your torso toward your right, as much as you can.
- Hold for 5 seconds by counting the numbers 2001 and 2002, 2003 and 2004.
- Gently and slowly return to your neutral position.
- Repeat the same motion by twisting your torso toward your left.
- 20 repetitions a day.

EXERCISES FOR THE BACK

Exercise 22 (Standing Wall Backward Leg Lifts)

- Stand facing a wall at arm's length.
- Gently raise your arm to touch the wall, with your hands and slightly rest your body against the wall.
- Gently lift your right leg backward
- Hold for 8 seconds by counting the numbers 2001 and 2002, 2003, 2004, 2005 and 2006.
- Gently lower your right leg and return to neutral position.
- Repeat the same motion with your left leg.
- 20 repetitions each day.

OPERATION STRONG SPINE

REFERENCES

Nachemson AL. Newest knowledge of lower back pain. A critical look. Clin Orthop 1992; Jun: 8–20.

Research on lower back pain and common spinal disorders. NIH GUIDE, Volume 26, Number 16, May 16, 1997, National Institutes of Health. Available from: http://grants2.nih.gov/grants/guide/pa-files/PA-97-058.html

José García-Cosamalón, Miguel E del Valle, Marta G Calavia,Olivia García-Suárez, Alfonso López-Muñiz, Jesús Otero, and José A Vega, "Intervertebral disc, sensory nerves and neurotrophins: who is who in discogenic pain?" Jurnal of Anatomy, 2010 July; 217(1): 1–15

Neil Osterweil, Robert Jasmer, "Acetaminophen Is Leading Cause of Acute Liver Failure" MedPage Today, Nov 30, 2005

Shereen Jegtvig, "Eating cues thrown off in people with back pain: study", Reuter Health, NEW YORK, Jan 15, 2014, www.reuters.com/article/2014/01/15/us-eating-pain-idUSBREA0E1A220140115

Darrin Pordash, Kari Riemann, Top Ten Chiropractic Techniques, Logan University, Dec. 1997

William J. Lauretti, What are the Risk of Chiropractic Neck Treatments? The American Chiropractic Association, 1996

OPERATION STRONG SPINE

Dvorak J, Orelli F. How dangerous is manipulation to the cervical spine? Manual Medicine 1985; 2: 1-4.

Jaskoviak P. Complications arising from manipulation of the cervical spine. J Manip Physiol Ther 1980; 3: 213-19.
Henderson DJ, Cassidy JD. Vertebral Artery syndrome. In: Vernon H. Upper cervical syndrome: chiropractic diagnosis and treatment. Baltimore: Williams and Wilkins, 1988: 195-222.

Terrett AG. Vascular accidents from cervical spine manipulation: Report of 107 cases. J Aust Chiro Assoc 1987; 17: 15-24.

Terrett AG, Kleynhans AM. Cerebrovascular complications of manipulation. In: Haldeman S., ed. Principals and Practice of Chiropractic. Norwalk, Ct.: Appleton & Lang, 1992: 579-98.

Jyrki Salmenkivi, Deaths due to medical error during spinal surgery are rare, Spinal News International, Oct 4, 2013

The case for personalized medicine, Personalized medicine coalition, 3rd edition

Grzanna R, Lindmark L, Frondoza CG. Ginger--an herbal medicinal product with broad anti-inflammatory actions. Journal of Medicinal Food. 2005 Summer; 8(2): 125-32.

Zi-Feng Zhanga, Shao-Hua Fana, Yuan-Lin Zhenga, Jun Lua, Dong-Mei Wua, Qun Shana, Bin Hua, Purple sweet potato color attenuates oxidative stress and inflammatory response induced by d-galactose in mouse liver, Food and Chemical Toxicology, Volume 47, Issue 2, February 2009, Pages 496–501

Sleigh, AE, Kuehl KS, Elliot DL . Efficacy of tart cherry juice to reduce inflammation among patients with osteoarthritis. American College of Sports Medicine Annual Meeting. May 30, 2012.

Kuehl KS, Perrier ET, Elliot DL, Chestnutt J. Efficacy of tart cherry juice in reducing muscle pain during running: a randomized controlled trial. Journal of the International Society of Sports Nutrition, 2010; 7:17-22.

REFERENCES

Daniel C. Cherkin, Karen J. Sherman, Andrew L. Avins, Janet H. Erro, Laura Ichikawa, William E. Barlow, Kristin Delaney, Rene Hawkes, Luisa Hamilton, Alice Pressman, Partap S. Khalsa, and Richard A. Deyo, A Randomized Trial Comparing Acupuncture, Simulated Acupuncture, and Usual Care for Chronic Lower back Pain, Archive of Internal Medicine. 2009 May 11; 169(9): 858–866, www.ncbi.nlm.nih.gov/pmc/articles/PMC2832641/

Margaret A. Nasser, Neurological Rehabilitation: Acupuncture and Laser Acupuncture To Treat Paralysis in Stroke and Other Paralytic Conditions and Pain in Carpal Tunnel Syndrome, Boston University

Burton AK, Tillotson KM, Main CJ, Hollis S. "Psychosocial predictors of outcome in acute and subchronic lower back trouble". Spine 1995, 20 (6): 722–8.

Dionne CE. "Psychological distress confirmed as predictor of long-term back-related functional limitations in primary care settings". Journal of Clinical Epidemiology, July 2005, Volume 58, Issue 7 , Pages 714-718,

An HS, Silveri CP, Simpson JM, File P, Simmons C, Simeone FA, Balderston RA. Comparison of smoking habits between patients with surgically confirmed herniated lumbar and cervical disc disease and controls, Journal Spinal Disorder. 1994 Oct;7(5):369-73.

Iwahashi, Masaki MD; Matsuzaki, Hiromi MD; Tokuhashi, Yasuaki MD; Wakabayashi, Ken MD; Uematsu, Yoshinao MD, Mechanism of Intervertebral Disc Degeneration Caused by Nicotine in Rabbits to Explicate Intervertebral Disc Disorders Caused by Smoking, Spine, 1 July 2002 - Volume 27 - Issue 13 - pp 1396-1401

Foreman, Stephen M.; Croft, Arthur C. (2002). Whiplash injuries : the cervical acceleration/deceleration syndrom. Philadelphia: Lippincott Williams Wilkins. ISBN 0-7817-2681-6.

Brent Bauer, MD, Mayo Clinic Wellness Solution for Back Pain, Gaiam, 2007

Ellis F. Friedman, MD, Outwitting Back Pain, The Lyons Press, 2004

OPERATION STRONG SPINE

John E. Sarno, MD, Healing Back Pain, Hachette Book Group, 2010

Webb R, Brammah T, Lunt M, et al. Prevenlence and predictors of intense, chronic, and disabling neck and back pain in the UK general population. Spine 2003; 28: 1195-202

Tim John Sloan, Rajiva Gupta, Weiya Zhang, David Andrew Walsh, Beliefs about the causes and consequences of pain in patients with chronic inflammatory or noninflammatory lower back pain and in pain free individuals. Spine 2008; 33 (9): 966-972

Stewart WF, et al. Lost productive time and cost due to common pain conditions in the US workforce. JAMA. 2003 Nov 12; 290 (18): 2443-54

H.R Guo, S Tanaka, W E Halperin, L L Cameron, Back pain prevalence in US industry and estimates of lost work days, American Journal of Public Health, 1999, July; 89(7): 1029-35

Relief for your aching back - What worked for our readers, The Consumer Reports Health Ratings Center, March 2013

Dr. Michael Peters, Dr. John Tanner, Eva Niezgoda-Hadjidemetri, Essential Back Care, DK Publishing, 2011

Keefe, F. J. (2011). Behavioral medicine: a voyage to the future. Annals of Behavioral Medicine, 41, 141-151

John E. Sarno, MD, Healing Back Pain: The Mind-Body Connection, Reed Business Information, Inc. 1999

Notarnicola A1, Fischetti F, Maccagnano G, Comes R, Tafuri S, Moretti B. Daily pilates exercise or inactivity for patients with lower back pain: a clinical prospective observational study. European Journal of Physical and Rehabilitation Medicine. 2014 Feb; 50(1):59-66.

Paul Little, et al. Randomised controlled trial of Alexander technique lessons, exercise, and massage (ATEAM) for chronic and recurrent back pain. BMJ, 337, August 19, 2008; www.bmj.com/content/337/bmj.a884

REFERENCES

Woodman JP1, Moore NR. Evidence for the effectiveness of Alexander Technique lessons in medical and health-related conditions: a systematic review. International Journal of Clinical Practice. 2012 Jan;66(1):98-112. doi: 10.1111/j.1742-1241.2011.02817.x.

Connors KA1, Pile C, Nichols ME. Does the Feldenkrais Method make a difference? An investigation into the use of outcome measurement tools for evaluating changes in clients. Journal Bodywork Movement Therapies. 2011 Oct;15(4):446-52. doi: 10.1016/j.jbmt.2010.09.001.

Lake, Bernard (1992). Photoanalysis of Standing Posture in Controls and Lower back Pain: Effects of Kinesthetic Processing (Feldenkrais Method sessions) in Posture and Gait: Control Mechanisms VII. eds. M Woollocott and F Horak, U of Oregon Press, , pp 400- 403.

Peng PW. Tai chi and chronic pain. Regional Anesthesia and Pain Medicine, 2012 Jul-Aug; 37(4):372-82. doi: 10.1097/AAP.0b013e31824f6629.

Hall AM1, Maher CG, Lam P, Ferreira M, Latimer J. Tai chi exercise for treatment of pain and disability in people with persistent lower back pain: a randomized controlled trial. Arthritis Care & Research (Hoboken). 2011 Nov;63(11):1576-83. doi: 10.1002/acr.20594.

Cramer H1, Lauche R, Haller H, Dobos G. A systematic review and meta-analysis of yoga for lower back pain. The Clinical Journal of Pain. 2013 May;29(5):450-60. doi: 10.1097/AJP.0b013e31825e1492.

Robert B. Saper, 1 ,* Ama R. Boah, 1 Julia Keosaian, 1 Christian Cerrada, 1 Janice Weinberg, 2 and Karen J. Sherman. Comparing Once- versus Twice-Weekly Yoga Classes for Chronic Lower back Pain in Predominantly Low Income Minorities: A Randomized Dosing Trial. Evidence Based Complement Alternative Medicine. 2013; 2013: 658030.

Nikoobakht, Fraidouni, Yaghoubidoust, Burri, Pakpour. Sexual function and associated factors in Iranian patients with chronic lower back pain. Spinal Cord. 2014 Apr;52(4):307-12. doi: 10.1038/sc.2013.151.

Ramsey S. Opioids for back pain are linked to increased risk of erectile dysfunction. BMJ. 2013 May 17;346:f3223. doi: 10.1136/bmj.f3223.

OPERATION STRONG SPINE

Ferreira PH1, Pinheiro MB, Machado GC, Ferreira ML. Is alcohol intake associated with lower back pain? A systematic review of observational studies. Manual Therapy. 2013 Jun;18(3):183-90. doi: 10.1016/j.math.2012.10.007. Epub 2012 Nov 10.

Ahn NU, Ahn UM, Nallamshetty L, Buchowski JM, Rose PS, Sponseller PD. Lumbar spine pathology and atherosclerotic risk factors: a 53-year prospective study of 1337 patients. TRANS AAOS, 68:155, 2001, The Spine Journal, Volume 2, Issue 2, Supplement 1 , Page 34, March 2002

Jerosch, Jörg; Heisel, Jürgen, Management der Arthrose: Innovative Therapiekonzepte, Deutscher Ärzteverlag. p. 107. ISBN 978-3-7691-0599-5.

Singh, Arun Kumar, The Comprehensive History of Psychology. Motilal Banarsidass Publ. p. 66. ISBN 978-81-208-0804-1.

Dickinson, John, Proprioceptive control of human movement. p. 4. Princeton Book Co., 1976, ISBN 860190021

Foster, Susan Leigh, Choreographing Empathy: Kinesthesia in Performance. Taylor & Francis. p. 74. ISBN 978-0-415-59655-8.

Brookhart, John M.; Mountcastle, Vernon B. Geiger, Stephen R. The Nervous system: Sensory processes ; volume editor: Ian Darian-Smith. American Physiological Society. p. 784. ISBN 978-0-683-01108-1.

Magnusson SP1, Simonsen EB, Aagaard P, Gleim GW, McHugh MP, Kjaer M. Viscoelastic response to repeated static stretching in the human hamstring muscle. Scandinavian Journal of Medicine and Science in Sports. 1995 Dec;5(6):342-7.

Taylor DC1, Dalton JD Jr, Seaber AV, Garrett WE Jr. Viscoelastic properties of muscle-tendon units. The biomechanical effects of stretching. American Journal of Sports Medicine. 1990 May-Jun;18(3):300-9.

Keitaro Kubo, Hiroaki Kanehisa, Yasuo Kawakami, Tetsuo Fukunaga, Influence of static stretching on viscoelastic properties of human tendon

REFERENCES

structures in vivo, Journal of Applied PhysiologyPublished 1 February 2001Vol. 90no. 520-527

Alan R. Stockard, Thomas Wesley Allen, Competence Levels in Musculoskeletal Medicine: Comparison of Osteopathic and Allopathic Medical Graduates, Journal of the American Osteopathic Association, www.jaoa.org/content/106/6/350.full.pdf, accessed on July 2nd, 2014

Kristina Åkesson, Karsten E. Dreinhöfer, A.D.Woolf, Improved education in musculoskeletal conditions is necessary for all doctors, Bulletin of the World Health Organization, 2003; 81(9): 677–683.

Oh DY, Talukdar S, Bae EJ, Imamura T, Morinaga H, Fan W, Li P, Lu WJ, Watkins SM, Olefsky JM, GPR120 is an omega-3 fatty acid receptor mediating potent anti-inflammatory and insulin-sensitizing effects, Cell. 2010 Sep 3;142(5):687-98

Dyszkiewicz A, Opara J. Monitoring the treatment of low back pain using non-steroid anti-inflammatory drugs and aromatic oil components, Ortopedia Traumatologia Rehabilitacja, 2006 Apr 28;8(2):210-8.

Sritoomma N, Moyle W, Cooke M, O'Dwyer S, The effectiveness of Swedish massage with aromatic ginger oil in treating chronic low back pain in older adults: a randomized controlled trial, Complementary Therapies in Medicine, 2014 Feb;22(1):26-33. doi: 10.1016/j.ctim.2013.11.002. Epub 2013 Nov 12

Yip YB, Tse SH, The effectiveness of relaxation acupoint stimulation and acupressure with aromatic lavender essential oil for non-specific low back pain in Hong Kong: a randomized controlled trial. Complement Ther Med. 2004 Mar;12(1):28-37.

Bahouq H1, Fadoua A, Hanan R, Ihsane H, Najia HH. Profile of sexuality in Moroccan chronic low back pain patients. BMC Musculoskeletal Disorders, 2013 Feb 15;14:63. doi: 10.1186/1471-2474-14-63.

www.ingramcontent.com/pod-product-compliance
Lightning Source LLC
Chambersburg PA
CBHW031950190326
41519CB00007B/739